DARK

DARK GLASSES

——

Blake Morrison

POETRY BOOK SOCIETY

Published in 1984 by
Chatto & Windus . The Hogarth Press
40 William IV Street
London WC2N 4DF

All rights reserved. No part of this publication
may be reproduced, stored in a retrieval system, or
transmitted in any form, or by any means, electronic,
mechanical, photocopying, recording, or otherwise,
without the prior permission of the publisher.

British Library Cataloguing in Publication Data
Morrison, Blake
Dark glasses.
I. Title
821'.914   PR6063.0793

ISBN 0-7011-2875-5

Copyright © Blake Morrison 1984

Photoset in Linotron Sabon by
Rowland Phototypesetting Ltd
Bury St Edmunds, Suffolk
Printed in Great Britain by
Redwood Burn Ltd
Trowbridge, Wiltshire

For Kathy

Acknowledgements

Acknowledgements are due to the editors of *Encounter,* the *London Review of Books, New Poetry 9, New Statesman, Poetry Review* and the *Times Literary Supplement,* where some of these poems (or earlier versions of them) first appeared.

'The Renunciation', 'Our Domestic Graces', 'Phone', 'Flood', 'Stepping in and out of Manet', 'Theory of Heredity' and 'A Concise Definition of Answers' appeared in Faber's *Poetry Introduction 5.*

'The Inquisitor' alludes to or borrows material from a number of sources, among them *The Book of Lech Walesa* (Penguin 1982), Rupert Cornwell's *God's Banker* (Gollancz 1983), *Bamm: Outlaw Manifestos and Ephemera 1965–70,* edited by Peter Stansill and David Zane Mairowitz (Penguin 1972), and Anthony Barnett's *Iron Britannia* (Allison and Busby 1982).

Contents

I

II

I

Pine

Growing up under the weight of wardrobes,
we have awarded ourselves pine. The old veneers
have been stripped away. A Swedish wife welcomes us
with her frank stare and enlightened ideas.

White wood, bright wood, your blonde shavings
fall away like the curls of a pampered child.
My fingers drift across the grainy fingerprints,
the dusty contours, the tumuli and cliffs.

Only these knots hold me, like some feud
from the past – the bad migraines
mother used to get, or a ridge of low pressure
swishing its cloudbursts on the childhood fête.

But we will chamfer all that. When you called
this morning I was clearing our old dresser
of its tea-rings and nicks, the yellow sawdust
heaping up like salt-sift in a glass.

It's a walk through sand-dunes down to the sea,
the space where honesty might begin,
if we knew how, no corners to hide in,
the coming clean of our loyalties, and lies.

The Renunciation

Our lives were wasted but we never knew.
There was such work to be done: the watch-chains
And factories, the papers to sign
In the study. Surrounded by brass
How could we see what we amounted to –
A glint of eyes as headlights swept away?

In a cot on the lawn lies my nephew,
Whose name I can't remember – the strands
Of family thinner each year, though we
Are here again, politely. The sun comes through
Like a faint reminder of things not done:
Forgotten dates, brothers not loved enough.

Peter, Jenny's husband, never forgave her.
When he caught them, out by the links, it was
All quite tame – some shouts and blows, Jenny
In tears, and the lover not showing again.
But later – well, Pete really cracked. Jen said he used
The affair as a way of opting out of things for good.

Here, on this stone, a relief map of lichen,
Each mossy headland like a lush green future.
Swallows gather on the wire, darkening
The air with their forked legends – journeys
We planned to take too, had the time been right
And the distance to the airport less far.

Every verse is a last verse, concluding
Sadness. You hear its tone in the chestnuts
And rookery – how much has been taken.
The garden with its nightshade nags like some
Vague guilt and the rooms look so untidy,
But there is nothing we know of to be done.

Simon has a sperm count of ten million –
Almost no chance at all, the clinic said.
'Funny those years of worrying if the girl . . .
When all the time . . . And now Louise, who'd set
Her heart on three at least . . . there's fostering, true, but . . .
I've lost the urge as well – know what I mean.'

I have learnt lately to admire the traits
Of those who dispossess me: their scars,
Their way of getting straight to the point,
Things mattering. Their families roam the orchards,
At home among the tennis courts and lupins.
I watch – I have resigned myself to light.

Our lives run down like lawns to a sundial
And unborn children play in a world I imagine
As good: the sash cords run free again
And I am leaning out and calling them
To hurry now and join us quickly, will they,
Quickly – we are all ready to begin.

Grange Boy

Horse-chestnuts thudded to the lawn each autumn.
Their spiked husks were like medieval clubs,
Porcupines, unexploded shells. But if
You waited long enough they gave themselves up –
Brown pups, a cow opening its sad eye,
The shine of the dining-room table.

We were famous for horse-chestnuts. Boys
From the milltown would ring at our door asking
Could they gather conkers and I'd to tell them
Only from the ground – no stick-throwing.
I watched from the casement as they wandered
In shadow, trousers crammed like mint-jars.

One morning they began without asking.
Plain as pikestaffs, their hurled sticks filleted
Whole branches, the air filled like a pillowfight
With rebellion and leaves. I was alone.
I had not father's booming voice. They were free
To trample through our peaceable estate.

Afterwards, matching father in a show
Of indignation (*bloody vandals and thugs*)
I imagined their home ground: the flagged backyards,
The forbidden alleys and passages
Winding up and out on purple moor,
The coal-sacks glistening in locked sheds.

It is June now, the chestnut scattered
Like confetti. He summoned me today
To the billiard-room – that incident
With an apprentice. *I've told you before.*
A son in your father's firm, you're looked to
For an example. I don't know what to do.

So I sit at my rosewood desk, lines fading
Across the parkland. I've been getting pamphlets
In a plain brown envelope and feel like
A traitor. Strangers have been seen
By the wicket-gate. Mother keeps to her bed.
English, we hoard our secrets to the end.

Long Days

Ph, this is nothing

His 'summer cold' is consumption.
Fog spills from the ocean
into his eiderdown and chest.
He reads by torchlight from Dowson
and Rossetti – those erotic,
nineteenth-century deaths.

The family won't accept it.
Since O'Neill gave him that opening,
papa's turned to drink.
Mummy under morphine imagines
she's a nun. Her orange-blossom
wedding dress lies mothballed in a trunk.

What if the sun came through?
There are dolphins at breakfast
but from then it's straight downhill.
The nights are the worst for him.
From the bottom of a whisky-glass
his brother says the most terrible thing.

He could still leave for the mountains
with their windchimes and zen.
But he's grown to love the fog,
it's like a sleep in the blue.
Even his stammer seems a part
of it, a not getting through.

At six he writes his journal
in the conservatory's cold.
The disease has taken hold.
Parts of me are chipping off.
I think God invented it to punish
the presumptions of the rich.

Foghorns thrum through dinner.
He wears a red-spotted handkerchief
to accommodate his phlegm.
It's veal again, and in the swirl
of the lighthouse he slides his plate back,
untouched. Wasting to the end.

Flood

We live in the promise of miraculous lakes:
Dagenham, Greenwich, Wapping, the Isle of Dogs.

'When the siren sounds, those in the blue environs
Should proceed immediately to non-risk zones.'

Spring tides, high winds: for days we can hear
Of nothing else, our eyes bright with disaster,

Our dreams a chronicle of *mountaing anarchie,*
The river-folke frantick, shippës trappt in trees.

And the dove we sent out, when it came back,
Had the brown glaze of estuaries on its beak.

In our dreams no sandbags hold back the flood:
We would bring the whole world down if we could.

Our Domestic Graces

The Chancellor of Gifts is an élitist.
You can't pretend he'll step out of the night
With a gilt invitation-card or flowers.
The brilliant words we wrote down in a dream
Aren't there beside our bedside after all.

Yet something calls from the great expanse
Of air we have made our latest home in.
Studio voices wake us near eight
With stories of God and how 'He moves among us
Constantly like light'. What are his tracks like?

Mystery starts no further away
Than these mossy footprints crossing the lawn
To where the raspberries are ripe again
And the panes of the greenhouse brim with tears.
Today even our lost city appears

From its shroud: a white dust-sheet slowly lifts
And here are all our glinting heirlooms –
The gasworks, like a coronet, queens it
Over the houses, and **bri**dges grace
The river with their lacy hems and Vs.

To have it all so clear – the congregating
Chimneypots, the lines of traffic passing
Over the heath like words being typed on a page.
Christ's fishermen must have felt like this,
Crying out, amazed, at their spangled catch.

Light falls about these rooms, silvering the face
Of what we are most used to, and ourselves,
Who on such days might think we had been
Elected at last – guest musicians
At the garden party of the gods.

A Child in Winter

Where is the man who does not feel his heart softened . . . [by] these so
helpless and so perfectly innocent little creatures?

Cobbett

When the trees have given up
snowberries come into their own,
winter grapes, albino
settlers of the dark.

With their milky blobs
they lined our doorstep
that November dusk
we swung your basket

up the gravel-path
and home. Child-Moses,
prince of the changing-mat,
heir of furry ducklings,

your babygros in drifts
on the clothes-rack,
we anoint your body's
rashes and folds.

When you cry it's like
some part of ourselves
breaking off and filling
these rooms with its pain.

Your breath's a matchflame
certain to go out,
we're at the cot hourly
holding our own.

In the shush of night-time
snowflakes crowd the window
like our own pale faces,
a shedding of old skins,

a blown seedhead,
paper pellets thrown down
by the gods to mark
your fiftieth day.

Lorries flounder on the hill.
We're out there watching
with a babysling
while the world goes under wool.

Little one, limpet,
resented stranger,
who has no time for me
and does not know time,

your home's the cradle
of a snowy hillfort
with pink turrets
and underground springs.

Daylight bores you: all night
you otter in our bed until
we wake to find you with us,
hands folded like a saint

accepting his death.
If it's we who must die first
that seems less costly now
having you here like wheat.

Spring comes, measured
in light and celandines
and your first tooth, faint
as a rock at low tide,

headstone for these trials
with cottonbuds and nappies,
your silver lips tracking
for comfort in the dark.

Stepping in and out of Manet

An untroubled nakedness:
the lady picnics
with these men from the city.

You were gathering violets
then took the rowboat
to the clearing where I waited.

There was a tree with fungi
like a frilly dress
and our lips' first meeting –

that wet little bridge of sighs.
Inhibition rolled away
like fruit across the grass.

Older now, framed in the doorway
to my study, you frown
to think how different we were

among the woods and cow-parsley,
where the light fell in
and our love was undisturbed.

Metamorphoses of Childhood

I

With my pair of labradors I lay
Like Romulus under the kitchen table.

We'll be back at six, my parents would say,
Abandoning me to the wolf-toothed nanny.

High above me her hands were baking
On a floured, unreachable shelf.

Later came squabbles with my fat twin-sister:
I was the handier, it seemed,

And to prove it constructed in days
A bakelite replica of Burnley.

II

The trains ran right through the middle of the house . . .
Well, almost: they were the giants in our hedge,

Breathing fire from their sooty toppers,
The burdens of the world on their back.

They were fetching for magnates:
Coal, cotton, shearings of quarry.

Cars queued up to hear them at the crossing.
Our teacups trembled on tenterhooks.

I pined for release from the attic room
Where a slip of the tongue had confined me.

III

Misery had no bedtime: it fell
Like lead in the middle of the night.

Boum, boum, boum, boum – it was the sound
Of boredom in my bloodstream,

The high room coming and going.
Why would the cornices never stay still?

First I was an elephant,
Then a pin in the infinite spaces.

Marapa, marapa, I'd cry,
But my parents never heard me.

IV

Where there's muck, there's brass they said,
As in the coppery shine of cow-pats.

But then I discovered the salt-lick,
A sort of blue whetstone lighting up the fields.

I'd been reading Scott Fitzgerald's
'The Diamond as Big as the Ritz'

And carried it home like a pools-win,
A sapphire from the mud. When I learnt the truth

It shrank in my grasp like an ice-pack:
I wept to be a prisoner of fact.

v

Death sauntered in adjoining rooms,
Familiar and airy as linen.

It was the dent in granpa's chair,
His saying *night-night* and never returning.

Heaven must be nice: his coffin
Looked plusher than a chocolate box.

And hell was just a nettle-sting
Or scorch from fireworks – only ages to heal.

Why, then, Daddy's tear, lying like a lens
On my new pointy-black shoes?

A Provincial Fiction

These fields are pale with the myth
of faithless sons gone south
to the 'airs and graces of the city'.

All's lost through the loss of them:
hands dwindle at the farm
and the woods are a sighing of chainsaws.

Doctor says there's little hope.
Will you be coming up?
We've kept your room just as it always was.

The stone fires, the piebald hide
of hillsides under broken cloud,
these grounds they had and will not go back on.

Meningococcus

'My son has gone under the hill.
We called him after a clockmaker
but God meets all such whimsy
with his early-striking hands.

That night of his high fever
I held a stream against me,
his heart panicky as a netted bird,
globes of solder on his brow.

Then he was lost in sea-fret,
the other side of silence,
his eyes milky as snowberries
and his fifteen months unlearned.

They have taken him away
who was just coming to me,
his spine like the curve
of an avocet's bill.'

Theory of Heredity

The generations come down on you –
like football crowds when a goal is scored.

It began when a sperm, waving its scarf excitedly,
tick-ticked its way in through the turnstile.

Now it's reached hundreds – parents, and their parents,
and the ones before that, stacked on the terraces

as high as sight, and you're at the bottom.
And when their tassels heave like a harvest-field

you will heave along, though you thought
by now you could go which way you pleased.

Transfusion

It is as we had always suspected:
God exists. Our scientists detected
His brain-rhythms while testing off Jura
For a new kelp-scheme on the ocean-floor.
Those North Sea oil-rigs are a cover.
We are drilling into the earth's core
To draw out his energy and breath.
We shall harness him to the body. Death
May very soon be a thing of the past.
War, famine, disease – they will be banished.
The sparrowhawk will mate with the ringdove.
We shall enter that garden where love
And all eternity lie in wait.

But for now God must stay our little secret.
Other nations cannot be trusted to
Accord him such reverence as we do.
Our own people, sad to say, are likewise
Unreliable. There would be chaos –
Rioting and looting in the street,
Panic at the thought of Him under their feet.
We must first construct a new theology.
Giving greater prominence to geology.
The Cabinet, in short, was unanimous:
For the present God's restricted to us.

This is my reason for summoning you
Here – to be added to the Chosen Few.
The operation, for anyone in doubt,
Is really nothing to be concerned about.

There is a specially constructed bunker
For a process we call 'aquapuncture'
Which releases God's spirit from a trapped nerve
And forces it upward through a large valve
Into pressure-cooled containers of juice.
By trepanning the skull we then infuse
You with the holiness of His brain.

There are, though, first some forms to fill in –
Life insurance cover, an IQ test,
Medical check-ups and all the rest
Of the usual but necessary irritations.
Please do your best to keep your patience,
And remember this: the lovely trance
Of what you will shortly experience
Will be eternal compensation. Are there
No questions? Then let us say this little prayer:

HYMN

(to the tune of 'The Trepanning Opera')

Oh, God, whose kingdom we tremble to come into,
Restore to wholeness our clapped-out bodies and minds.
Our eyes are heavy as leather purses,
Our brain-cells are feverish as a wasps' nest,
Our hearts are massing with cholesterol choirs,
Our blood clogs the gutter of every continent,
And we are full of piss and wind.

32

Oh, God, we see at last how unseeing we have been:
Your fingerprints are whorls in the seabed,
Your nails the glacial mountain lakes,
Your knuckles the peaks on an ordnance survey,
Your buttocks the cleft of all-knowing,
Your teeth just the tip of an iceberg,
Your pores the space between clouds.

Oh, God, forgive us for not reaching you earlier,
Whose hair is the corn-glow of the prairies,
Whose brow the curve of the earth,
Whose sweat the sheen on playing fields,
Whose breath the fog down the Pacific,
Whose mouth the chasm in the solar system,
Whose penis the miracle in the bush.

Oh, God, though we are worthless and ridiculous,
Let us drink the rainfall of your irises,
Let us lodge under your fingernails like sand-grains,
Let us eat out of your palm like gazelles,
Let us strap-hang in your nostrils like pollen,
Let us sit on your tongue like communion wafers,
Let us make our living in your heart.

And now, God, we can feel you seeping into us,
We can hear you singing in our veins,
Each tissue is restored like an oil-painting,
You surge in our arteries like a rip-tide,
Our lungs are bigger than the universe,
The old rhythms are changing, here is love
Like a volcano in the roof of our heads.

Oh, God, this is my transfusion,
I must keep you here forever,
I will surround myself with sentry-posts,
I will hug you to my bloodstream like a bantam,
I will kill any man who tries to take you away.
This is my possession. This is my religion.
This is the meaning of God.

Ice

In a white room with chessboard lino
Beatrice interrogates a tumbler of ice.
Wait, wait, she has it clear at last:
The skylit boxroom where her husband
Meets another to become less squarely himself.
She can see them stand, filmed in sweat
And with sheets around their navels, like
The brothers Alberti, 'cramponed breast to breast'.

I was there till eight at the Institute,
If you had only called. Miss Talleyrand,
The one who sees hell as a vagina,
Had been led by she-wolves through a kingdom
Of ice. It was a classic quest-myth –
Mazes, mages, tricks with double mirrors –
And when they reached the throne there was mother
Chained to the father and gnawing out his eyes.

But she will not believe this, having heard it
All before. His trembling thumbs press down
On the ice-tray until it gives like a neck-cord
With two little puffs of breath. Poor phantoms,
Held there in prisms of despondency,
I'm here to see you make it up again,
To warm to your theme-song of treachery
And suspicion, so different from my own.

Phone

Somewhere a phone was ringing – perhaps for you.
It sang like a chance that would change the world,
Though the room, when you got there, seemed undis-
    turbed,
Dust and sunlight for a hundred years
No noise had ever got under.
It bothered you for a while, but friends came round,
And the summer was a deep, deep blue
That stretched over mountains and marram-grass
And paved terraces with drinks at sunset.
They were beautiful hours, weren't they,
High and open as Alpine fields where even the cows,
Belled and indolent, sound musical.
You should have forgotten but it came back –
What the voice would say if you caught it in time,
Something on a line you did not recognise,
Though the tone seemed familiar and the background
Rushed forward like a shower of bright coins.
Well, you went on: there was no one to say
It would not ring again or in time maybe
That you couldn't dial yourself. These nights draw in,
Misty light fading by four, but the words
At least will be burnished when they come,
Like *Why not meet me?* or *I forgive you.*

A Concise Definition of Answers

The city calls with its arches and spires
While the flatlands flourish with incest.
There are more curious things I wanted,
If possible, to touch on today –
How the sky, for instance, on these sultry afternoons
Seems to settle round your forehead,

Or the link between nostalgia and smell.
At this point science comes in, as you might expect,
Or as you might yourself come in with that
Colander of raspberries and rain. It seems like
Everything we hoped for, as if the mayor had cut the tape
And events might finally begin.

But look, there's a storm blowing up, the sky
Flickering like an old TV and the volume
Almost deafening. Answers: I was holding them here
Just now but they are gone again into those
Cloud-lit days where martins and swifts sweep low
Over the ground but can turn up nothing.

Dark Glasses

And take upon 's the mystery of things
As if we were God's spies . . .
King Lear

The privacies of lace and leylandii.
The pseudonym to climb through like a trap-door.
The dark falling as you enter what was said
In the summer-house, behind the Chubb,
Beyond the entryphone, inside the glass-topped wall.
What nestled through customs in a hub-cap.
What you must never mention to anyone.
For God's sake, Harry Lime, hold your tongue.

Or this other sort, let's-be-candid-please,
Big Mouth, the soul of indiscretion,
The gust that took the trellis clean away.
This Norfolk skyline, vast and open-hearted,
Levels with its questioners, or seems to,
For though we left with a full confession
By the time we played the tape back that evening
It had reverted to a row of noughts.

Either way you come out none the wiser.
She is silky and elusive, returns
At twelve dripping beads from a broken necklace,
An accident, a little job for you
(A job to ignore the flush in her cheekbones
And the departure of a misted car).
And this – how you love it – is mystery,
Wrapping itself around you like a bride.

But something cries out to be resolved.
The pen moves off with its search parties.
There are footlights on the dipped horizon,
As if the ones whose plot we are part of
Were on the brim of coming clear. It's late
But they'll be here by nightfall, you know they will.
Just as you despair their red torches
Flash through the dark like fluke late raspberries.

II

We had among us, not so much a spy,
As a recording chief-inquisitor . . .
                    Browning, 'How It Strikes a Contemporary'

He had repeatedly hid himself, he said, for hours together behind a bank at the seaside, (our favourite seat,) and overheard our conversation. At first he fancied, that we were aware of our danger; for he often heard me talk of one *Spy Nozy*, which he was inclined to interpret of himself, and of a remarkable feature belonging to him; but he was speedily convinced that it was the name of a man who had made a book and lived long ago. Our talk ran most upon books, and we were perpetually desiring each other to look at *this*, and to listen to *that;* but he could not catch a word about politics.

                    Coleridge, *Biographia Literaria*

I am Cinna the poet, I am Cinna the poet . . . I am not Cinna the conspirator.

                    Shakespeare, *Julius Caesar*

The Inquisitor

I THE TASK

What trust would be like they never explained.
The eye of a deer miles away in woodland,
Children running at the edge of a town . . .
But this was not their way of talking.
In a panelled room in an annexe
To the ministry they laid down all the terms.
Knowledge is death. Trust no one, least of all
Friends. Loyalty? There are some secrets here
So terrible we keep them from ourselves.

So they gave you Finland, which was OK
At first but then it got boring. Contacts were scarce
– They had tightened the borders and the Gulf –
One sad Estonian, straight from Le Carré,
Who shared with you ham omelettes, beer and *frites*.
You worked from home, mostly, the cottage
By the kalefields. Rachel, you were sure,
Was having her first affair and you'd return
From Helsinki unannounced, hoping to surprise her.

There were times it felt like someone's dream
Your own had got snared up with – the lies
To be told *for the sake of the country,*
The endless undertones like schoolboys
Whispering in class. The weeks billowed
Around you like a huge tent, roomy with light.
You leant back in the captain's chair
And got no further. The cases proved
Intractable or turned out not to count.

Then came the call from the Director.
You do not smoke but watch him tapping
His cigarette against the silver case.
Your wife, yes, and children? He gazes down
To where the Thames and its bridges glitter
Like a cold-frame. *A special job's come up.*
Someone arrived in London yesterday
We think may be of use. Be careful, now:
Only scholarship will help you to survive.

But you must wait, you have been told you must
And the paper they give you is just bumf.
The officials at their desks, light through
A venetian blind lining them like notepads,
Are engaged in lies. The text is for the enemy
While you proceed with oral tradition
In the outposts of the nation – a racecourse,
Perhaps, or unpatronised bar, will bring
The muttered codeword from a stranger.

And the men, when they speak, are not reassuring:
Scrabbling clerks, Pegasus bikeboys, stoolies
And sneaks, princes of the cubbyhole
And keyhole, neighbours charged with an exquisite
Sense of duty, whose trade is the tip-off
And the unsigned note, who want no part
And don't appear in the acknowledgments page,
From whose sleek antennae nothing escapes,
The anonymous company of God –

And whose anonymous company you keep.
Today's one, trilby worn low as an eyeshade,
His collar's V deep as a railway cutting,
Turned from the river to proffer two names:
Treslowa, Binjon. But where are these to take you?
Ironic light seemed to play about his eyes.
Even the reeds might seem to whisper
The betrayal of a king. There is nothing
In the river but reflection and waste.

II THE PRICE

The Senior Tutor has lent you his typescript
On 'Masculine Imagery in Donne'.
It would embarrass you to say so
But it lacks somehow the brilliance
Of his conversation. Tact, then – silence is best.
The college garden blossoms with tongues.
End-of-term dances, tennis at midnight,
The summer solstice – you know even now
It can't go on like this, there's a price to pay.

She was just twenty-one, nice enough.
Left to itself it might have lasted six months.
But now this third ghosted beside you,
Wrapped in a lucid mantle, crouched, hooded,
You cannot tell yet whether man or woman
(You dare not think whether yours or another's),
Only that morning in the oasthouse
Laying to rest the panic and reproaches:
By now even the fingernails are formed.

45

So this was love, like Lady's Slipper seeding
Despite itself, a podburst of confetti
Settling on the mourners by the churchyard gate.
You hardly know her but her body's changed
Already, her nipples darkening to blue.
You bask in the cool of the canal-bank.
You inhale the breath of freezer-shelves.
You spread guide-books on a table, where by the end
Of August your Europe is covered in dust.

Straightening and re-shaping a paperclip,
The Senior Tutor sounds faintly appalled.
He's kept his windows tight all summer.
Donne has been revised: *I make this link between
The hurrying-on of the comma'd line-ends
And the seducer's haste — it's going to rattle
All the Griersonites*. Coaxing the blind half-down
He keeps his back to you: *No luck, I'm afraid,
With your fellowship, but something else . . .*

That winter McAlpine cranes laboured and spun.
High above the classroom men in yellow helmets
Strutted round like Hannibal on the Alps.
You were fitting children for offices,
Their heads bowed, their biros toeing the line,
Something to tide you over. Rachel's mind
Seemed to have gone completely. She moved about
Like some long-legged seabird, plumaged with
The babythings she'd smother at her breast.

The child came early and was delicate.
He lay under his cloche like a frail plant,
Seemed certain to die. Those nights in the hothouse
You cannot think straight or be sure of anything
But this ward of animal terror,
The authentic image of the world . . .
Until your son comes home at last, wall-eyed,
His silky skull throbbing like a hamster's,
A stranger and intruder, whom you love.

The ghosts of the smoky staffroom affect
To be delighted by the news. They mistrust
Your appointment. They observed you observing.
That trick of saying nothing when the knives
Are out at tea-break has brought you both fear
And prestige. You're friends with three women
Who feel like stones at the tidemark – cold, hard,
But with that silkiness underneath.
And with Maclelland, guerrilla of the text:

The horses in this poem, with their manes
Of iron, symbolise a challenge to the state.
Their 'dinned hooves' are the drums of revolution.
They have thrown their jockeying leaders.
They are like gods hiding in the outfields
Of the system, the beautiful ones
Who will return to set the ghostly cities right.
'Whinnying with rage', as the poet puts it,
They feel the power within them to stampede.

Harmless, no doubt, but Fitzroy loves it,
Glubbing a Highland whisky in your glass.
Donne? He's had no time for Donne of late,
What with reviewing fiction for the *TLS*
And re-reading the Russian classics
(*A stick to beat the new boys with. Have you read
John Fowles? I can't believe he's any good.*)
It's all there in his drawer of index-cards,
The names of the infamous on its tongue.

Another drink? Yes, you will need another
Before disclosing any more. Come, come,
You must not think of this as treachery:
They are children playing near the flames
Of history who need protection from themselves.
The names are unimportant, a matter
Just for us and these four walls. And in exchange
The formal letter, dropping like destiny
Into the stained glass puddle of your hall.

If this were art you might despise yourself
And confide to notebooks a squalid poetry
Of excuse. But this is verse without the end-stops.
Last night was your entrée to the meeting-house:
Trots, feminists, fugitive professors,
Ex-cobblers, martyrologists and Beats,
They welcomed you with Maclelland and spoke
Of the attempt on the Observatory
And the Conrad assignation next week.

And Rachel and Ben? You'll do your best
To keep them out of this. Today, from your desk,
You see her climbing the hill with him,
A plastic carrier-bag lumpy with
New vegetables wedged inside the pushchair.
They move so painfully, with his hanging back
To gather stones and grass-blades, you've to step
Out of the lamplight and hurry down
To meet them, your family, the one clean thing.

III TOPPING

There is a murder, as there has to be . . .
Scarpe grosse, cervello fino – his stealth
Was learnt in the hills of Valtellina.
He kept his head down and his books clear.
He took the long train to the Russian front,
Served with diligence, ate his mount in the snows,
And developed a taste for iced vodka.
Then he returned to make his fortune
In the banking cathedrals of Milan.

'When two people know a secret it is
A secret no more' – this was his motto,
And he was good at drawing secrets out
Of others while not giving away his own.
He makes a pact with the Vatican
But learns his trade from the *sottobosco,*
The heirs of Garibaldi, who swear him in
On the back seat of a Mercedes
With the ritual of the masonic sword.

49

He rises to be Baron of the Treetops
And can see the gilt Madonnina
As he swivels his rosary-studded chair.
His office is vast and triangular,
With bullet-proof windows, a private lift
And eight gorillas posted at the door.
They say he sends aid to Solidarity.
On his antique desk he keeps a bottle
Of mineral water, nothing more.

Dietro ci sono le tonache —
The cassocks are backing him to the hilt.
A shiny nameplate and a telex machine
Have spread the word to the Bahamas.
It keeps on spreading — Luxembourg, Zurich,
Panama, Antwerp, Liechtenstein, New York.
He has nothing to give beyond a promise
But the next life is always about to happen
And the faithful buy enormous shares.

Until the police come like sceptics to dispute
In detail his Calvinist heresies and shams.
The Vatican stops its letters of comfort.
The organ-grinder flees, leaving only his monkeys.
Bruciato — ruined in an hour,
He descends to the dumb-show of the trading-ring,
The mania of tick-tack men, and knows he is done.
He moves with a lucid desperation
Like his hurt secretary falling through air.

Assegno delle sette – the dawn arrest,
And the release on bail. He goes in retreat
To his converted barn at Drezzo,
Feeding documents to the wood-burner,
And consoling himself with the works of Poe.
His two marremani sheepdogs howl like babies
As the nightwind infiltrates the door.
He eats a plate of cold chicken, then goes –
Klagenfurt, Innsbruck, Lake Constance, Gatwick,

To the divan in Chelsea Cloisters
Where the *Loggia di Londra* will help.
But time is in the night like a hunter.
He shaves his moustache of a lifetime.
He turns the lock of his overnight bag
To its open sesame – O-O-O-O.
He takes his last effects – a black finger-glove,
A passport in the name Calvino,
And a cellophaned bank-wad of francs.

He stands above the unfamiliar streetlights
And waits for the door to knock, a friend's knock,
Though a friend with needles and a motor-launch,
The act timed to perfection on the high tide –
For there has to be a murder, or suicide –
Ten pounds of masonry in his turn-ups,
The nylon-rope with two half-hitches
His feet washed in the river by the Churches
St Mary Somerset and St Bride.

'There is no comfort, only resignation.'
At the memorial service in Drezzo
The mourners are outnumbered by bulbs.
God's banker is dead, though it's said his desk-lamp
Shines like an angel on the top floor.
What is the faith that others live by?
Who came for him and why? Gold, speculation,
The unmaking of men made by the pledge that
Anything they say so is true – solve it, you!

IV TAILING

If the clouds took up dust as they do water
They would rain the blood of those we loved.
London Bridge on a weekday morning,
The dark commuters gathered like filings,
And the one among them you must track
Like a compass to the arms of Dominant House.
You're the last of the great biographers,
Living in the echo of his footsteps,
The recording minister at his back.

Mist rises from the helipads and piers,
That Gothic swirl you've seen in old films,
When light comes off the pavement and the air's
A lift from Turner, implying all it hides.
They have found a second body under Blackfriars Bridge:

Is that the way he means to take you,
Through the dripping gullies and fur-halls,
A moth in the tenements of the mink trade,
A masked diver on the river's cobbled floor?

A blackbird dips down the alley, freak
Of the City as foxes are and daffodils
Or The Hatchet buried by Lippy Furs.
He is leading you into history,
Past Zachary Gillam and the beavers
Of Canada, whose tracking and trapping
Concluded here as pelts in a warehouse,
The hunters contracted out before you,
Their legacy the blood-rust of the Thames.

V A MESSAGE FROM POPOWO

You have parked in the silence of hedgerow
And grass – bramble, foxglove, white convolvulus
With its spirals and bowls. Though you're concealed
There's a clear view of the lane and for an hour
Only a beer-waggon has passed, with its corral
Of rattling stock. But you're uneasy:
It's like that carriage on the night train,
Tobacco smoke fresh in the corridor,
An invisible waiter at your back.

The names are in your ears of all the lost
Adventurers, your peers, this one forthright,
That one sly, all of them now departed:
Taylor dying on the road from the airport,
Neilson who went mad on the underground,
Aspinall mauled, Boudin blown to bits –
Lost, lost! In a sheet of flame you saw them
And you knew them all, the world's true masters,
Its chief inquisitors, if the world but knew.

Then the car draws up and he steps towards you
With his carved walking-stick and broad-brimmed hat,
'Herr Mettich', in sandals (as you'd heard)
And a signet-ring sealing the handshake.
He takes his place beside the driving seat
In time for the afternoon eclipse,
The smoked window rising like a curtain
On his monologue, the only light a circle
In the dashboard glowing for cigarettes.

'Let me tell you what it is like to find
A man in our century. You have his name
But that's invented. No fixed address.
A chameleon of the identikit –
Tall, short, dark, fair, moustached and clean-shaven.
Here's his photo, surely, on a picket-line
Or is it here as ambassador to Rome?
No schoolfriend has seen him for fifteen years
And they ask for a report by next week.

'But I've his birthplace and the district,
Fifty miles by a hundred. Popowo?
The yellowing map shows a fertile plain –
Windmills, watermills, apiaries and hops,
A thousand hamlets tiny as pinheads . . .
But this Popowo, it's been abolished, clearly,
A landslide has carried it from the page.
I had to drive out one October dawn
Under a sky shadowed with migrations,

'Moss heavy on the trees, the roads slippery
With cattle-dung and elm-leaves, to the silence
Of the spas. Here the people keep their heads down,
They hoard their secrets like fairy-rings
Past Lisek, Fabianki, Swiatkowinza,
Past barns, smallholdings and stagnant ponds,
Until by chance comes a township, Popowo,
And a village doctor certain in his mind
Yes, a child of that name was born here.

'But he's alone: no-one can recall the boy.
Days are squandered on the parish register
And nights in the company of cranks.
The black-dressed women washing linen
At the pump smirk over my impudence –
To ask such questions of the likes of them!
But, wait, the name's vaguely familiar,
A cousin who stayed during wartime – yes,
The family came from Chalin way, not here.

'Rain again, time passing through the drenched willows,
The wipers tocking like metronomes, until
At Chalin I learn – a miracle! –
Popowo's three miles south. *Another* Popowo,
Where the chief clerk will personally
Direct me to the 'family seat', here
Past the lime pit and the hardened cement-bags
To a bricked-up cowshed set among plums.
So this is all. He can see my disappointment –

'Will I not join him for supper, it would
Delight him to dine with me, a man of such
Refinement and tact. But my interest
In that family, frankly he's surprised –
Common folk who owned three hectares and a cow,
The father stirred up trouble, was caught stealing
Newspapers from the big house – a rough lot,
Certainly. They say the boy's now high in
Government – should one believe it or not?

'At the school, a wooden mansion-house
Long cobwebbed from disuse, the bearded caretaker
Rises from her rocking-chair to furnish reports.
It might be said of almost anyone:
A diligent student of Class I B,
Ran the 100 metres in 11.6,
Walked about with his head bare, smoked a lot
And was a likeable sort of bully,
A good organizer, left in '61.

'Here it goes dark: his parents are dead,
No teacher or officer can recall him,
There's just the one letter to a schoolfriend,
With word of a job in engineering
And that he'd taken a flat near the Cathedral
For which he paid 800 zloty a month.
He is waiting in the shadows for history
To invent him, the 'little corporal',
Remembered, if at all, as a card.

'So I returned to my superiors
And told them this man was a nonentity,
Nobody to worry us in the least.
But that disruption at the shipyard?
His speech from the top of a telephone booth?
Put it down to his youthfulness.
Lenarciak, Suszek, Gwiazda, Nowicki –
These were the ones to keep an eye on,
This other just a ghost out of the sticks.

'You have guessed, of course, as you would have to:
This was Walesa, or soon to be,
There before my eyes yet wholly missing,
A face between nowhere and everywhere,
Unfathomable as the workings of *Vlast*.
What hope for you, then, in your own quest?
Better write the history of a raincloud
Than think one can ever know a man,
Or tabulate the measures of his heart.

I tell you this to save you disappointment.
I'll do my best to help: you must speak to Razumov,
Who's made a clean breast, and to Kregraink.
Much beside the point can be accomplished.
But the task you have set yourself is hopeless,
A plot leading nowhere, a dark game
To distract you from knowledge, like the wind
Through beeches keeping us with its promise
There is more to it, more to it, than this.

VI THE PILLOW BOOK

You debate with a man from Penguin
Evolution in a finch's beak.
You are full of haws and fossil-saws.
He prefers the explanation of God.
Around you mild and torpid monsters
Settle for oblivion, more or less.
The celebrities have left for l'Escargot.
You're stuck with the passengers of alcohol,
Taking their seats on its nightly express.

Then the tide recedes from the Galapagos
And you are left with her alone. *Eva,*
She smiles, and offers a hand to you,
And lets you fill her wineglass several times.
These publishers' parties — so dull, dull.
It was too obvious, but you're already
In the taxi, stepping North past Regent's Park
And Primrose Hill — to the glow of her bedstead,
Her braceleted arm turning out the light.

How many evenings have ended like this:
To wake at dawn under a vaulted ceiling,
The sweet anonymities of one a.m.
Reverting under the thin light to guilt,
Loathing, fear of what a turned shoulder
Will bring – though it brings, whether freckled or dar]
Roughly the same: cracked lips, encumbered breath,
Her dryness, yours. What was it kept you, then?
There was that nervousness at breakfast:

Fresh orange-juice, white lies and reassurings.
She seemed impatient, as they always do,
Showed you the door . . . which opened, though, on t]
The bed again, her dress on the floor like a shadow,
The green minutes of the digital clock
Mounting inexorably as your breath.
She knows you'll be late for your appointment
But, wait, she must give you this – her Union,
To enter freely, come and go at will.

Weeks riffle past under an open window
Like the pages of her Taoist guide.
What is your preference today? The tiger's tread?
The mountain goat facing a willow?
The feast of peonies or the pair of tongs?
These mysteries of cloud and rainfall,
Like the passages no censor can excise:
'Stroking my hair, she moaned like Circe
As I buried my new beard between her thighs.'

Today, an hour with the Director
To present your returns. They are quite worthless
And he tosses his personalised golfball
With an air of disdain. *Let me be frank,*
Old chap. There's been some pressure from above –
A deal with the Americans, it seems.
He takes his putter from the filing tray,
Stooping over it as if to say grace.
I'd say another week is all you have.

Afterwards, at Gaston's, you are tempted
To confide. Her eyes across the table
Appeal to you for candour, her hand
Now rests in yours. But where would be the point?
It is not what you want with her anyway,
But to tip the chauffeur handsomely
And drive at once to some remote wood
Behind the smoke of an official car . . .
Next day's a Friday and the August weekend:

You escape with her up the motorway,
Its lamps curving their necks as if to sip,
Swan-like, from the rushing passage of life,
Or as arms might join above your head
For the bright arch of a wedding-dance.
In the hotel she takes four ribbons
From her bag: *One day I must start wearing them,*
But now, please, darling . . . The Prisoner
Of Sex – it is a game she loves to play.

For hours you're awake with that special tiredness –
Driving, the insoluble, and love.
Whose sweets were those in the glove compartment?
What did Karl mean by *the quieter room upstairs*?
Movement of arms by night – pairs of tail-lights
Slipping down the road into another country,
Or would it be by plane? She stirs beside you.
There are sounds across the mere like owls
Or churchbells – it's impossible to say.

And there are wakenings more like wish-dreams
Or death: to fight up from the oceanbed
And find her mouth on yours, her pouring hair
As if you'd stepped behind a waterfall,
Her navel's mirror reflecting your own.
Breath matched by breath, you're like those mad twins
Who speak each other's every word and thought,
The air still bristling with electricity
As she pulls on her silky green dress.

And so you tell her, since it seems she must know:
Over cider, in the sunlit garden
Of the Cockpit, she sits indifferent
Through your narrative and this annoys you
So you tell her, very slowly, again.
The world should open up but there is only
The flutter of crisp-packets. Driving back
To London, buffeted by cross-winds
From juggernauts, it's as if she's failed some test.

*Quels bons bras, quelle belle heure me rendront cette région
d'où viennent mes sommeils?*

Rimbaud

This is the excitement that ends in pain.
Dark names stretch for you from their seedbed,
Bronze statesmen harangue the crowded squares.
All week you've driven round the capital
In a blacked-out Volvo, testing the way.
What is this new air, ideas run up flagpoles,
The people pressing to some grand conclusion,
Not to be restrained. It seems to lead
Straight to disaster, or to lunch with Lascelles.

It was his job to let the Empire die,
But it dug in. Telegrams came from islands
It was thought were long since sold, their morse
A sandpiper weeping over lost inlets
And strands, those Northern coastlines like the hand
Of a delegate pleading at the UN
*Send out your forces and deliver us
From pain. We were at one with the sheep
And cormorant until the soldiers came.*

Those cadences cost him his job. After
The bad reviews, the bayings for blood,
And then the blood in the bay to meet them,
He resigned, seeking consolation in
Restaurants, where he'd amuse himself
In strategies with a wineglass and two forks
Or the global policing of a melon.
These brought a navy made of toothpicks
Cascading off Columbus's earth.

Today, years on, the world does not remember.
He's there in Bertorelli's, as they said
He would be, at the same corner-table,
With neither greeting nor smile. His drink's
Martini, since 'it reminds me of Martinez,
You know, de Campos, the Spanish general,
Deposed for his leniency in Cuba.
I have become, you see, since my demise,
An expert in the scapegoats of Empire.

'They sent you, I know, for what I can tell
Of the nation: *j'ai seul la clef de cette parade*.
Our leader dreams of bringing the Great back,
Her Jerusalem's made of sterling,
Her voice rings like a grocery-till, softened
With the pity she's hardened from the land.
Her grail's religious: coming from the flatlands
She dreams of death on a high green hill.
Nothing can countermand the Iron Will.

'And yet she's tapped the English heartland'
(This, as the waiters he's grown old among
Scurry to the portholed door, which swings and swings
Like an unfastened boom in a gale,
And the heaped promise of each silver dish
Is carried to the white-beached archipelagoes
Then returns with its skeletal remains:
Backbones, legbones, shoulderbones, brain –
And there are some still champing to be served)

'We are an island in love with the idea
Of islands, of a marooned people,
Helpless as seal-pups, crying for their lives.
Our hearts go out to them, we are authors
Of a pastoral for the powerless,
Protectorate of all shepherds and kelpers,
Our Empire of Seaweed encircling the weak
On their windswept promontories of light.
So we succour and oppress, who might have slipped
From history unnoticed as the auk . . .'

But he's exhausted and drunk, the sentence
Unfinished as he motions you to leave.
Your driver is waiting in Charlotte Street,
Your journey back by tomorrow's parade-route
Down Shaftesbury Avenue, the Strand and Ludgate Hill.
Scarlet hangings have gone up on the houses,
The new vision will be met with in tunes
Whose stern injunction, culled from ancient hymn-books
Is to ransom the captive and *rejoice*.

At the Church of St-Andrew-by-the-Wardrobe
You ask the car to wait. The Observer's
Behind you, the God long since renounced
Is sulking still, and silent, but there are whispers
From the vestry, where the choir are arranging
Their cassocks and hair. It's your image of trust –
The altar-stairs sloping through darkness,
Children filing to the East window who sing
To perfection what they cannot understand.

And your report? Forehead to penthouse window,
You have your last view of the nation,
The river of a darkening capital
And its diamond clusters of self-love.
You could write now of good misdirected
And innocence betrayed, but the deadline has come,
Only the foghorns wail like creatures from
Prehistory: *Speak to us, who cannot see
Where we are going or know what is right.*

VIII CANENS

You pick the children up at ten and drive them
East to Dunwich, a coastline they're too young
To remember, the city under the sea
Where nothing of what happened remains.
You ask them (in passing) how their mother's been –
She was looking drawn, you thought, and they speak
Of her tiredness and headaches. Right, past the church,
You follow the B road to the Bird Reserve,
A wind from Holland streaming through the hides.

The marrow in her bones was dissolved
By sadness and she wasted in air.
It's said the sources are always one
And the same. *Ovid, ibid* go a pair
Of reedlings by the mill on Walberswick Marsh.
Your heart contracts to nothing as you consult
The drawing in your Child Ornithologists' Guide:
The male plump on freshwater molluscs,
The female sheltered under his rufous wing.

And her old letter, marking the entry
For *picus viridis,* the green one and its mate:
I believed in you. To survive as we did
Early on, and then a second child and third:
I grew to think of it as an achievement.
It was your going away that changed it,
Not the affairs themselves but the knowledge
I'd been living with an imposter.
It is all, you see, a question of trust.

This is how ghosts begin, the ash of memory,
White hawthorn and the mild-frothed river,
The milky shards she dug from the berberis
Out of someone else's past, as if this mist
Were the breath of the land's dead labourers,
The yeomen and marshmen, the husbands
And husbandmen, the sowers of seed
Among flint and hummocks, gathering barley
While the North Sea cantered at their back.

And the cottage by the kalefields that year
After Finland: they had frozen all posts
And for a summer you lived there unoccupied
Getting every detail by heart – the beads
She wore, the swing under the apple-tree,
The vine, the sandpit, and the hinged lid
Of the nesting-box that was always going
To reveal some featherbedded circle
Of happiness, but somehow never did.

You call them back to you, like a moorhen
With her bleeping chicks across the furry stream.
These reeds go down to where the beach begins,
A sandstone cliff-edge wearing into nothing,
Less and less each year, as there is less and less
Of her, a drained fen, a voice in a millstream
Trying not to reproach, trying to keep
The children from its whispered briny song:
Yes, we were happy – but only for so long.

IX LET IT GO

Whose are the steps behind you in the hall
Though the wet marble holds only your own?
Who is the son of straw? Whose warnings
Carry in the wind, where the lamp breaks up
And the mirror can no longer hold its stare?
Your protégé is working at your desk.
There are skeletons in the filing tray.
They've acknowledged your review but consider
Its conclusion *the product of an overstretched mind.*

Leaves rush towards you like peasants fleeing
A napalmed village of the East. It has
Something to do with you – but what exactly?
When you slide the study window up
Papers blow about the room and you must kneel
Among them like somebody in mourning,
Names staring up as if from gravestones
Buried in the grass: Horovitz, Jeffares,
Casey, Lorne – faces you'd prefer to forget.

And the answer they want, would it be dull?
A name you rejected weeks ago?
Having the air of what you were supposed
To think? Or just less feasible than most?
The questions recede like hyacinths
Then return with waxy clarity each dusk.
You're relieved to need no longer pursue them:
A plumb-line to the mud, a body
In the river with each fingernail extracted,
That's how the lost identities turn out.

'The conspiracy of our spacious song':
In your dream last night the elms along
The ministry drive seemed to part for you.
The passes had been passed, on a high floor
The final room was waiting, the answer
In a file marked NEVER TO BE OPENED.
It solves the world: there is a great party.
Eva, who is God, descends from the boardroom
To present you with a case of severed heads . . .

You see her next morning at the cottage
Under the whish of an Icelandic wind.
The garage OPEN sign spins like a coin.
A fine spray is chiselled from rainbutts.
The swallows have gone from the outhouse,
Painted warriors recalled to their wattle huts.
While she talks to you with emphasis
A white powder like cocaine or cow-parsley
Trails its ashes from a bag of cement.

She is sorry to have been elusive –
She's been so busy, so very busy of late.
But this time spent apart has not been wasted.
She's come to recognise how things were
So much better before they became too intense
(Yes, like standing at the edge of the town's
Most exclusive party, not daring to go in).
What she means, to put it brutally, is
That *it's over, but we had best stay friends.*

She will have supper, please, you want her to
(For there's a question left to ask). Roast lamb,
Red wine, something gingery with windfalls
You'll choose the instant by the mantelpiece,
Her face lit by the rush-burn of seasoned pine:
By the way, I met a friend of yours,
Said he once worked with you in Milan . . .
And she admits it by not hearing
As she pulls you quickly to her one last time.

A solution of sorts, though the fields
Deny it, returning a wintry blank.
The harvest tractor with gulls in its wake
Has departed the way of all stubble,
The days are short, the last of the tourists gone.
Only the mole persists with its cottage industry,
There beneath the lawn could you but see it,
Laying its sponge-roads and puffy veins,
Its working life all channelled to one end.

There are no ends, though, and no answers, for this
Is secrecy, whose art it to withhold
The logic it is richer not to know.
The word at large behind the berberis
Cannot be caught, not quite. The padlocked gate
Stays padlocked and we cannot trust our sense
Of what was happening through its iron,
The child in search of a blackened tennis ball
Who stumbled on a crossbow and a throat.

Now is the right time to surrender –
As in the weakening December light
One is suddenly thankful for the fourth stroke,
Scone-time and the flicking on of headlamps:
At last one can drop all pretence of effort –
Laying a path, dictating a letter,
Or the task of deciding what we are
And where we come from – well, it's too late for that
And (anyway) no longer seems to count.

Your connection is waiting in the street.
One day he will ask to deliver a message
And the porter 'forget' that he must not.
Aren't those his steps in the hallway now?
They have given him a key, then. His face,
There will be time and all time to observe
In passing its passing resemblance to your own.
And his voice, like a playback of your voice:
This is going to feel precisely like death.